My Journal

Collecting Thoughts

This book belongs to

_____

_____

_____

2021 Cover Art © by Iva Dukić

Iva Dukić is a painter and illustrator from a small historical town in Croatia. She graduated at the Academy of Applied Arts in Rijeka where she began working on her first projects in children's books illustration.

After participating at Malik, Festival of myths and legends in 2012, where she worked on illustrating characters from stories and legends, she began to take an interest in mythology and folklore and that continues to be a big influence in her artistic expression in the future.

She likes spending time in nature and often finds her inspiration when riding her mare through the forest.

Her work is based on dreamy and mystical landscapes filled with animals and little forest creatures. The purpose of her art is to inspire and encourage children and adults to free their imagination and dreams.

Till now she illustrated several books for children and she participated in various exhibitions and events.

Contact: zmamorije@gmail.com

ISBN: 978-0-578-90547-1

Positive Thoughts
Positive Mind
Positive Life

Positive People
Positive Places
Positive Life

Remember to be... Amazing

Content

Authentic

Balanced

Basic

Beautiful

Courageous

Courteous

Astonishing

Curious

Tranquil

Expressive

Determined

Devoted

Creative

Encouraged

Energetic

Enthusiastic

Excited

Great

Fabulous

Giving

Eager

Happy

Dedicated

Joyful

Kind

Loyal

Neat

Nice

Optimistic

Positive

Humble

Punctual

Radiant

Reliable

Resilient

Savvy

Serendipitous

Simple

Sparkly

Spontaneous

Steadfast

Supercharged

Terrific

Thankful

Timeless

Virtuous

Dazzling

Unique

Valuable

Versatile

Virtuous

Wise

Wonderful

Writing

Youthful

Zany

Zestful

Amazing

Astonishing

Understanding

Balanced

Basic

Beautiful

Courageous

Courteous

Creative

Curious

Dazzling

Dedicated

Determined

Devoted

Eager

Encouraged

Energetic

Enthusiastic

Excited

Expressive

Fabulous

Giving

Great

Happy

Humble

Joyful

Kind

Loyal

Mindful

Authentic

Nice

Optimistic

Positive

Prepared

Punctual

Radiant

Reliable

Resilient

Savvy

Serendiptious

Simple

Sparkly

Spontaneous

Steadfast

Supercharged

Terrific

Thankful

Timeless

Tranquil

Understanding

Unique

Valuable

Versatile

Zany

Wise

Wonderful

Writing

Youthful

Powerful

Zestful

Intentional

Exceptional

Considerate

Steadfast

Writing

Happy

Powerful

Thankful